What Is Light?

Exploring Science with Hands-on Activities

Richard and Louise Spilsbury

Enslow Elementary

an imprint of

Enslow Publishers, Inc.
40 Industrial Road
Box 398
Berkeley Heights, NJ 07922
USA

http://www.enslow.com

Enslow Elementary, an imprint of Enslow Publishers, Inc.

Enslow Elementary® is a registered trademark of Enslow Publishers, Inc.

This edition published in 2008 by Enslow Publishers, Inc.

Library of Congress Cataloging-in-Publication Data

Spilsbury, Richard, 1963-
  What is light? : exploring science with hands-on activities / Richard and Louise Spilsbury.
      p. cm. — (In touch with basic science)
  Summary: "An introduction to the properties of light for third and fourth graders; includes hands-on activities"—Provided by publisher.
  Includes bibliographical references and index.
  ISBN-13: 978-0-7660-3097-8
  ISBN-10: 0-7660-3097-0
  1. Light—Study and teaching (Elementary)—Activity programs. 2. Optics—Study and teaching (Elementary)—Activity programs. I. Spilsbury, Louise. II. Title.
  QC365.S65 2008
  535.078—dc22
                    2007024550

Printed in the United States of America

10 9 8 7 6 5 4 3 2 1

For The Brown Reference Group plc
Project Editor: Sarah Eason
Designer: Paul Myerscough
Picture Researcher: Maria Joannou
Managing Editor: Bridget Giles
Editorial Director: Lindsey Lowe
Production Director: Alastair Gourlay
Children's Publisher: Anne O'Daly

Photographic and Illustration Credits: Illustrations by Geo Ward. Model Photography by Tudor Photography. Additional photographs from istockphoto, pp. 10, 16; Shutterstock, pp. 4, 6, 18, 25.

Cover Photo: Tudor Photography

contents

WHAT IS LIGHT?

Light is a kind of energy. We need light to see things. In a totally dark room we cannot see anything.

Some objects give out light. They are luminous. The Sun, our nearest star, is luminous. It is a very hot ball of burning gas. The Sun is the main source of natural light on Earth. Artificial sources of light include electric light bulbs, candles, and computer screens.

Bright Light

The amount of light a luminous object gives out depends on how bright that object is. A candle flame only spreads its light a few yards. The Sun is about 92 million miles (148 million kilometers) away from Earth, but it is so bright that it lights up our world.

▼ *As the Sun rises over a city, it casts long shadows from the buildings.*

CLOSE-UP

SHADOWS

Shadows are seen when an object blocks the path of light rays. The size of the shadow depends on how close the object is to the light source, and how big or strong the light source is. The closer an object is to the light source, the larger and more blurred the shadow is.

● When the light is farther away from an object, the shadow it makes is smaller (top). When the same light is close to the object, it makes a larger shadow (bottom).

Light on the Move

Light normally travels along straight paths called rays until it hits an object. Light can travel through transparent materials, such as glass. Materials that light cannot pass through are opaque.

When light hits an opaque object, a shadow appears on the other side of the object. Because light cannot curve around the object, the light is blocked and a shadow forms.

REFLECTIONS

When you look in a mirror, or at the surface of a lake on a sunny day, you can see reflections. The clearest reflections happen when light rays bounce off flat, shiny surfaces.

All objects reflect light, but some reflect light better than others. Flat, shiny surfaces reflect light rays well. A mirror produces a clear image because it reflects nearly all the light that hits it.

When light rays hit uneven, dull surfaces, the rays bounce off in all directions. They cannot make clear reflections. When sunlight travels through the atmosphere, it bounces off tiny particles in the air and spreads out to light up the sky.

CLOSE-UP

REFLECTION IN A MIRROR

When an image is reflected in a mirror on a wall, it is flipped from left to right. Wink at yourself in the mirror with your left eye— your reflection will wink back with what appears to be the right eye!

Mirrors

A mirror usually reflects almost all of the light that hits it. Most mirrors are made of a flat sheet of glass covered on the back with a thin layer of a shiny metal, such as silver or aluminum. Behind the shiny metal is an opaque material. Light hits the mirror from the side you are on, and is reflected back to your eyes. You see a reflection of yourself and the room behind you.

◀ *Objects reflected in a lake appear to be upside down!*

Make a Two-Way Mirror

Can a mirror work on both sides?
Follow these steps to find out.

SAFETY TIP

The edges of the piece of glass may be sharp, so handle it very carefully. Ask an adult to help you cover it with Mylar and tape the edges.

1 Ask an adult to help you cover one side of the glass with the Mylar film. Make sure the film lies flat against the glass.

You will need

- piece of glass about 1 foot (30 cm) square • sheet of Mylar™ (antiglare window film) big enough to cover the glass • cloth tape and scissors • 2 electric lamps • large pieces of modeling clay or several books

2 Carefully tape the film to the edge of the glass with the cloth tape. Use more tape to cover the edges of the glass.

3 Put several large pieces of modeling clay on the bottom of the mirror and use them to stick the mirror to a table. You can support the mirror with books if you do not have modeling clay.

4 Make the room dark and position one lamp on each side of the mirror. Ask a friend to sit on one side of the mirror while you sit on the other side. Switch on one lamp. Then switch it off. Do the same with the other lamp. Then switch both lights on at the same time.

WHAT HAPPENED?

You saw a reflection of your face when only your lamp was switched on. This is because when your friend's light was off, very little light passed through the mirror from the other side, and nearly all the light you saw in the mirror was reflected from your side.

When your light was off and your friend's light was on, you saw your friend's face in the mirror, perhaps with a very faint reflection of your own. This happened because your side of the mirror was dark, and more light was coming through from the other side. When both lights were on, you saw only your own reflection.

BENDING LIGHT

When you look at a straw in a glass of water, it seems to bend where it enters the water. That happens because light refracts, or bends, as it passes from the water to the air.

Light refracts because it travels at different speeds through different transparent materials. When light moves from one substance to another, its speed changes. For example, when light travels from air to water it slows down. When light hits the water at an angle, the change in speed also makes the beam of light bend.

◀ *Rainbows form when billions of raindrops act like tiny prisms.*

COLORS OF LIGHT

Light from the Sun and most light bulbs may look white, but it is really made up of different colors. This range of colors is called the spectrum.

A prism is a piece of glass with triangular ends that divides light into its separate colors. Each part of the light ray refracts by a different amount as it passes through the prism, creating the different colors we see. Violet rays bend the most and red rays bend the least. The other colors are in between.

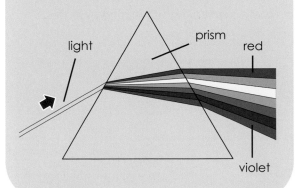

light prism red violet

Light Speeds

Light travels fastest in outer space—at up to 186,500 miles (300,000 km) per second. It takes about eight minutes for light from the Sun to reach Earth.

Light moves slightly slower through air, slower still through water, and even slower through transparent solids, such as glass.

Trapped Light

Sometimes light gets trapped inside a material such as glass or water. If an underwater diver shines a flashlight up toward the surface at a shallow angle, the light reflects back down under the water instead of escaping into the air.

Slow Down Light

Does light travel differently through different objects? Try this experiment to find out.

You will need
- 2 glasses ● pitcher of water
- cooking oil ● baby oil ● 2 glass stirrers
(or other small, clear glass objects)

1 Place one glass on a table in a bright place, but make sure there is no strong beam of light coming from just one direction. Pour water into the glass until it is about a third full.

2 Carefully pour a thick layer of cooking oil on top of the water.

3 Fill half of the second glass with baby oil.

4 Place one glass stirrer in each glass. Look at the glasses from the side. What can you see? Are some parts of the stirrers fainter than others?

Try doing the experiment using corn syrup instead of baby oil. The stirrer will appear to vanish, because light passes through corn syrup at the same speed as it passes through glass, so it passes straight through the stirrer without being bent.

WHAT HAPPENED?

You should have noticed that the glass stirrer became faint, or even disappeared, where it passed through the cooking oil. It should have been easier to see in the baby oil.

The light bends most as it passes into and out of the stirrer in air. It bends a bit less when the stirrer is in water. The stirrers are hardest to see in the oils because light bends relatively little when it passes through oil. That is why the stirrers appeared so faint.

Trapping Light

Did you know that light can be trapped? Find out how.

You will need

- glass tank full of water • milk
- bright flashlight with a narrow beam
- washable felt-tip pen
- protractor • ruler

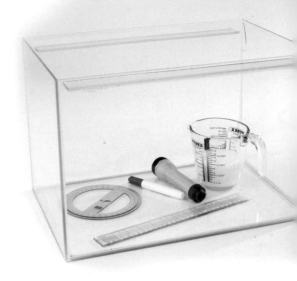

1 Clean the tank carefully, then fill it with water. Pour in a little milk. You should still be able to see through the water. Make the room dark.

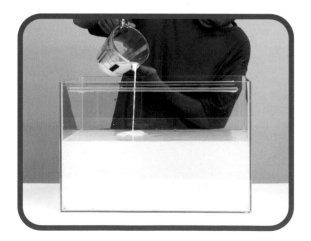

2 Shine the flashlight through the side of the tank. Angle the flashlight so that the beam hits the water surface from below. Is the light reflected down, or does it escape into the air? Or do both things happen?

WHAT HAPPENED?

The angle between the vertical line and the sloping line should be about 49°. This is called the critical angle. When the angle of incidence (the angle at which light hits the water) is greater than the critical angle, the light reflects off the water instead of passing through it. It bounces back under the water, and is trapped there.

3 Move the flashlight until you find a position that makes the beam shine along the water's surface. Ask a friend to use the washable pen to mark the beam's path to the water's surface with a series of Xs on the front of the tank.

4 Draw a line through the Xs with the ruler. Then draw a vertical (straight up-and-down) line through the point where the angled line meets the water surface.

5 Use the protractor to measure the angle between the vertical line and the sloping line.

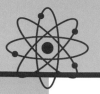

LIGHT IMAGES

Sight is one of our senses. We see images when light reflected off objects enters our eyes. Our eyes see an object as a pattern of light and dark in different colors. Our brains turn this pattern into an image we recognize. Cameras are machines that record light images we can look at.

How Eyes Work

Near the front of the eye there is a black hole called the pupil. Light from an object enters the pupil and passes through a transparent part called a lens. The lens refracts light from different distances away onto a layer inside the back of the eye called the retina.

The optic nerve carries the image from the retina to the brain so that you can "see" it. After passing through the lens, the image on the retina is actually upside down. The brain turns this image the right way up again.

CLOSE-UP

A LIGHT-SENSITIVE LAYER

The retina can be damaged by very bright light. The eye controls the amount of light that enters it by changing the size of the pupil. The colored iris is a circle of muscle that can change the size of the pupil's opening.

If you look in a mirror in a bright room and then in a darker room, you might notice that your pupils have changed from smaller to larger!

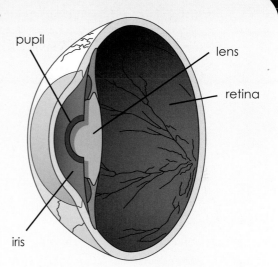

Cameras capture images in a similar way to eyes, but they can also store the images so lots of people can see them.

Taking a Picture

A digital camera works something like an eye, but instead of a retina it has a light sensor. This sensor is divided up into tiny squares called pixels. Light from the scene you are photographing travels through the lens and strikes the sensor. Information about the light hitting each pixel is pieced together into a complete image by a mini computer inside the camera. When you take a picture, the image is saved onto the camera's memory card.

17

USING LENSES

People use lenses in optical instruments such as eyeglasses, binoculars, and telescopes. A lens is a piece of transparent glass or plastic that makes objects look bigger or smaller.

▼ *A magnifying glass has a convex lens that increases the size of the object you are looking at.*

A lens works by refracting light rays. The center of a convex lens curves outward. Light rays entering the lens from one side refract toward the center, so they come together on the other side of the lens. When you look through a convex lens, nearby objects look larger. A concave lens curves in toward the center. It makes light rays spread apart, making objects look smaller.

Focal Length

The point at which all the light rays come together after passing through a convex lens is called the focus. This is the point at which a clear image forms. The distance between this spot of light and the lens is called the focal length.

CLOSE-UP

HOW LENSES WORK

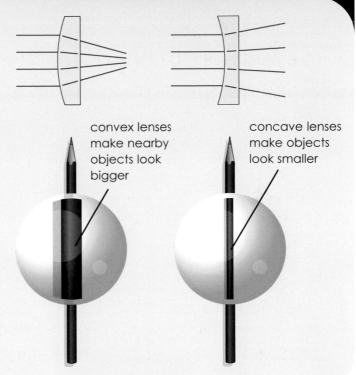

A convex lens focuses light rays into its center. That makes things that are up close look bigger. Eyeglasses with convex lenses can help farsighted people see nearby things more clearly.

A concave lens spreads out light rays. That makes objects look smaller. Eyeglasses with concave lenses can help nearsighted people see far-away objects more clearly.

convex lenses make nearby objects look bigger

concave lenses make objects look smaller

Optical Instruments

Microscopes use several convex lenses together to enlarge an image by a greater amount. They can make really tiny objects big enough to see up close. Telescopes collect light from stars and planets millions of miles away and use several lenses to make the images big enough for us to see.

19

Fishbowl Lens

Did you know that water can act as a lens? Discover how with these simple steps.

You will need

- round glass bowl • water
- candle • dish • piece of thick white cardboard • ruler

1 Fill the bowl with water. This is your lens.

SAFETY TIP

Ask an adult to light the candle. Keep the cardboard away from the candle at all times.

2 Place the candle on a dish about 1 foot (30 cm) away from the lens. Ask an adult to light the candle.

WHAT HAPPENED?

The bowl of water acted as a lens. Light from the candle bent as it passed through the bowl. As light passed from air to glass, it hit the glass at an angle and refracted. The light bent again as it entered the water, then passed through the center of the bowl.

When the light passed out into the air on the other side it refracted again, but this time it bent in the opposite direction because the light was passing into air. The focused image of the candle on the card was upside down.

3 Hold the cardboard against the bowl on the opposite side from the candle.

4 Gradually move the cardboard away from the bowl. Stop when you see an image of the candle flame on the cardboard. How does this image compare to the real flame?

Refracting Telescope

How can a lens magnify an image?
Try this experiment to find out.

SAFETY TIP

Ask an adult to help you use the knife. And <u>never</u> look at the Sun or any other bright object using a telescope, because the light can damage your eyes.

You will need

- 2 cardboard tubes, one that fits tightly inside the other • several convex glass or plastic lenses wide enough to cover the end of each tube • ruler • sharp knife • tape and scissors

1 Hold a smaller lens near your eye and a larger one at arm's length. Move the larger lens closer or farther away until you see an object in focus. This will be the length of the finished telescope.

2 Measure the distance between the lenses. Cut both tubes to about two-thirds of this length.

WHAT HAPPENED?

The length between the outer lens and your eyes is the focal length of the telescope. This is the distance the large lens needed to focus light from the object through the small lens onto your eye. The small lens magnified the light image so your eye could see the object clearly.

3 Tape the larger lens to the end of the wider tube.

4 Tape the small lens on to one end of the narrow tube.

5 Slide the end of the narrow tube without the lens into the wide tube. Point the telescope toward a distant object. Looking through the narrow tube lens, slide the wide tube away from your face until you see the object in focus.

23

LIGHT WAVES

Waves spread out when you throw
a pebble into a pond. We can think
of light as traveling in waves, too.

Waves move up and down as they travel in a
particular direction. The highest point of a wave is its
crest and the lowest is its trough. Wavelength is the
distance between two crests or two troughs. Amplitude
is the height of a crest or the depth of a trough.

When Waves Meet

The effects that happen when
waves meet are called interference.
Sometimes the crests combine to
make waves with double the
amplitude. Sometimes the crest
and trough cancel each other out.

Each of the colors that make up
light has a different wavelength.
So when light waves meet,
the colors mix and produce
new colors.

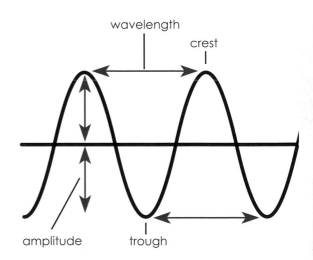

Soap bubbles look colorful ▶
when light waves reflect off
them at different angles and
interfere with each other.

CLOSE-UP

DARK AND LIGHT

Light shining from a single source can diffract to make a pattern of light and dark bands. The light bands are places where two passing crests combine and create a wave of greater amplitude. The dark bands are places where a crest and a trough of two waves meet and cancel each other out.

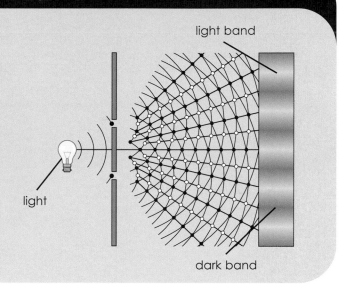

light band

light

dark band

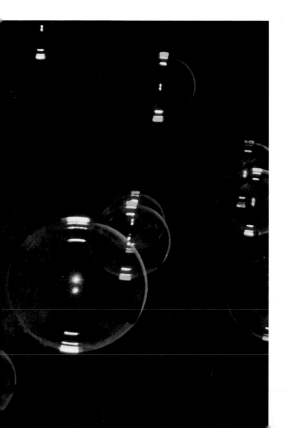

Spreading Waves

Light waves spread out, or diffract, when they move through a very narrow space. If there are several spaces for the light to pass through, the diffracted light waves combine and interference happens. We see this interference as patterns of different colors from the light spectrum. Scientists use a machine called a spectrometer to diffract different kinds of light and study the spectrums they produce.

Rainbow Patterns

How is a rainbow formed?
Follow these simple steps
to find out.

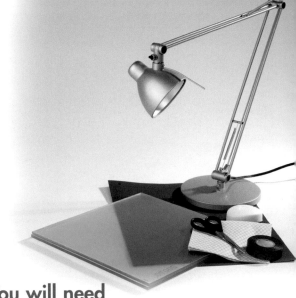

1 Clean both sides of the Plexiglas pieces with soap and water. Rinse, then dry with a soft, clean cloth.

2 Press the squares of Plexiglas tightly together. Hold them in place while an adult helps you to tape the edges together.

You will need

- 2 pieces of Plexiglas™ (acrylic glass) about 1 foot (30 cm) square and about ¼ inch (3 mm) thick • clean cloth
- soap and water • tape and scissors
- piece of dark paper • desk lamp

3 Tape the black paper to one side of your Plexiglas "sandwich."

4 Hold the Plexiglas sandwich, papered side down, under a bright desk lamp. You should see rainbow patterns in the Plexiglas.

5 Carefully bend the Plexiglas sandwich. How do the rainbow patterns change?

WHAT HAPPENED?

The colored pattern you saw in the Plexiglas was caused by interference. The white light from the lamp reflected off the bottom of the first sheet and off the top of the second sheet of Plexiglas. The two sets of reflected light waves interfered with each other across the thin air space between the sheets. That caused the rainbow.

The patterns changed when you bent the sheets because the width of the space between the sheets was changed. The angles at which the light was reflected toward your eyes was also changed.

Make a Spectrometer

Can you separate the colors in light? Find out by making a spectrometer.

You will need

- shoebox with lid • tape and scissors
- construction paper • fine-mesh window screen • lens • flashlight • colored pencils
- white paper • modeling clay

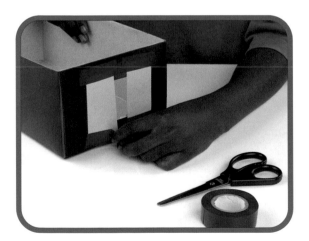

1 Cut a 2-inch (5-cm) square in each end of the shoebox. Tape two strips of construction paper over one hole, leaving a very narrow vertical slit between them.

2 Carefully cut three pieces of window screen and overlap them unevenly, so that the mesh holes are partly blocked. Beware of the sharp edges of the screen.

3 Hold the screen "sandwich" over the slit and look through the screen toward a light. Twist it around slowly until you can see colors. Tape it into place over the slit.

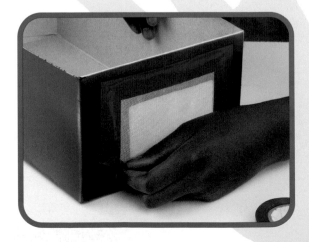

4 Put the spectrometer on a table and tape the lid on to the box. Lay a sheet of white paper near the mesh. Shine the flashlight from the other end of the box. Move the lens in front of the mesh until the spectrum appears clearly on the paper.

5 Use a piece of clay to hold the lens in the position where the best spectrum shows. Copy the spectrum onto the paper using the colored pencils.

WHAT HAPPENED?

The lid on the shoebox kept out light from all sources except the flashlight. The light from the flashlight was diffracted by the slit and the mesh, and the spaces were small enough to spread the different wavelengths of light apart into a spectrum. You focused an image of the spectrum onto paper by positioning the lens at a particular distance from the slit.

GLOSSARY

amplitude—Height of a wave's crest or depth of wave's trough.

concave lens—Lens that curves in toward the center.

convex lens—Lens that curves outward in the center.

diffract—When a light beam bends or spreads out.

focus—Central point at which rays of light meet after being reflected or refracted.

interference—The way light waves change when they meet. When light waves meet, some colors cancel each other out and others get stronger.

iris—Round, colored muscle around the pupil in the eye. It can change the size of the pupil to control the amount of light that enters it.

lens—Clear part of the eye that focuses light rays onto the retina. An artificial lens is a transparent object that refracts (bends) light.

opaque—Describes material through which light cannot pass.

prism—Transparent object that bends light to break it down into the colors of the rainbow.

pupil—Round, black hole in the center of the iris in the eye. Its size can change to control the amount of light that enters the eye.

refract—Describes the way light rays bend when they pass from one kind of material (such as water) to another (such as air).

spectrometer—Machine that diffracts light to create a spectrum.

spectrum—Range of colors seen when light passes through a prism.

transparent—Describes material that light can travel through. You can see through something that is transparent.

wavelength—Distance between two neighboring crests of a wave or two neighboring troughs.

FURTHER READING

Books

Nankivell-Aston, Sally, and Jackson, Dorothy. *Science Experiments With Light*. New York: Franklin Watts (2000).

Parker, Steve. *The Science of Light: Projects and Experiments with Light and Color*. Chicago, Ill: Heinemann (2005).

Tocci, Salvatore. *Experiments with Light*. New York: Children's Press (2002).

Internet Addresses

Light-Science.com
www.light-science.com/agesto12.html

Optics for Kids
www.opticalres.com/kidoptx_f.html

The Science of Light
www.learner.org/teacherslab/science/light

INDEX